Steps to FORGIVENESS

A Walking Beyond Series Book

Karen Todd Scarpulla

Little White Dog Press

Copyright © 2013 Karen Todd Scarpulla

All rights reserved. No part of this book may be reproduced, stored in a retrieval system or transmitted in any form or by any means without the prior written consent of the publisher, except by a reviewer who may quote brief passages in a review to be printed in a newspaper, magazine, blog or journal. Requests for permission should be sent to:

Karen Todd Scarpulla: Karen@walkingbeyond.com

This is a self-help book and contains some autobiographical elements about the author. The author has made every attempt to recreate events, locales and conversations from her memories of them. In order to maintain their anonymity, the author may have changed or may have left out the names of individuals, places and identifying characteristics and details such as physical properties, occupations and places of residence.

This book is not intended as a substitute for the medical advice of a physician. The reader should regularly consult a physician in matters relating to his/her health and particularly with respect to any symptoms that may require diagnosis or medical attention.

PUBLISHED BY LITTLE WHITE DOG PRESS

ISBN-10: 0989158934
ISBN-13: 978-0-9891589-3-0

First Edition

INTRODUCTION

In my book, *Walking Toward the Light, a journey in forgiveness and death,* I share my story of learning to forgive my ex-husband in the last year of his life. At that time, I was his primary caregiver while he died of esophageal and stomach cancer. My experiences during those 12 months altered the course of my life and changed me profoundly.

When I learned of his diagnosis, I made the decision to move in with and care for him so that our two children would be able to spend valuable time with their father.

We had lived apart for six years, so naturally moving back in brought up old family dynamics, and I began to experience feelings of anger and sadness. I tried to convince myself that I had forgiven him. Certainly, I must have forgiven him. How else could I possibly make the decision to care for him? It wasn't long before my emotions were running high. I was desperate to find forgiveness. I needed to stop all the negative feelings I was having. They were affecting my physical well-being.

At first, I turned to the internet to search for articles and books that might help me with the process. Most of the advice I found encouraged the use of mantras as a way of instilling forgiveness. I tried this method; however, daily mantras were not enough for me to overcome years of "bad" feelings. I knew I needed something more, so I developed my own plan to forgive.

I am passionate about sharing this process. We have all been in positions in which we have been hurt, wronged or abused at some point in our lives. In order to grow, we each must heal from these experiences. The key to healing is forgiveness. It is the first step.

Steps to Forgiveness outlines the process I used to forgive and heal. The process itself is simple, but working through the emotions and embracing the journey may be challenging. Work at your own pace. When you experience resistance to an idea in the book, I encourage you to take a break and let your mind and body process what you have read. Remember, the more you resist something in your life, the more you think about that very thing. Such thinking will lead you to attract more of what you are trying to avoid. Try to keep an open mind. After all, what do you have to lose? The gains will be immeasurable. My hope is that these steps will help you find your own path so that you can experience the power of forgiveness and the strength, peace and grace it brings.

TABLE OF CONTENTS

CHAPTER ONE
    WHAT IS FORGIVENESS..................1

CHAPTER TWO
    WHY SHOULD I FORGIVE..............3

CHAPTER THREE
    FORGIVENESS BEGINS WITH YOU..............6

CHAPTER FOUR
    STEPPING STONES TO FORGIVENESS 11

CHAPTER FIVE
    IT'S IN YOUR ACTIONS..................18

CHAPTER SIX
    FEEL THE POWER..............21

CHAPTER SEVEN
    FORGIVENESS AFFIRMATIONS..................23

RESOURCES..24

"The weak can never forgive. Forgiveness is the attribute of the strong."

—Mahatma Gandhi

If you are reading this book, you have taken the first step toward forgiving. It all begins with the overwhelming desire for change and taking that initial step.

CHAPTER ONE
What is forgiveness?

*"Forgiveness is a funny thing.
It warms the heart and cools the sting."*
— William Arthur Ward

The dictionary defines forgiveness as "the willingness to cease to feel any resentment against someone. To absolve, to grant pardon or give up all of your judgments and claims for this individual. To let go of the pain, anger and resentment caused by an event or offense."

I describe forgiveness as the process of letting go of anger, bitterness, resentment, and the old movies that play in our minds and keep us from moving forward in our lives. Forgiveness is the ability to completely let go of the act that has created the pain.

You stop judging the offender and release yourself from the hurt. When you reach this state of true forgiveness, you will feel empowered. Your heart will feel full, the weight will be lifted from your shoulders, and your body will feel light. I have experienced forgiveness as not only an emotional state of being, but as a physical state, as well.

There is a misconception that forgiveness means reconciliation with the individual who has hurt you and that forgiveness is equated with condoning his or her actions. Forgiveness does not mean that you approve of the behavior or offense. You are simply releasing yourself from the emotions tied to the event.

I was worried that if I forgave my ex-husband, he would take this as a cue that we could be in an emotional relationship again. Living together was difficult because people treated us as if we were a couple, even though we were not. I was so afraid to let him in emotionally because I feared being hurt. These thoughts were major stumbling blocks on my path to forgiving him. I was fearful that he would use my forgiveness to begin pressuring me to build a relationship. Instead, I discovered that my forgiveness was all about me and my emotions.

Forgiveness does not mean that you need to build any kind of connection with the person you are forgiving, especially if there has been no change in his or her behavior. I think this one misconception is a pitfall for many people on the road to forgiveness.

Of course, forgiveness can sometimes help mend a relationship, but only if the person you are forgiving has experienced true change. By forgiving, you create the power to decide whether this person is allowed in your life or not.

CHAPTER TWO
Why should I forgive?

*"Forgiveness does not change the past,
but it does enlarge the future."*
— Paul Boese

We have all had the experience of someone hurting us. When someone does something to you that is so horrible that it violates your boundaries, it can compromise your belief system and shatter your faith. You become adamant that there is absolutely no way you will be able to forgive him or her. Your story about the traumatic event completely justifies your actions of never forgiving this person. After all, how could you forgive someone who hurt you so much? The anger and resentment you feel is deep, and your heart is wounded. I know how it feels. I have been there.

Constantly living with these emotions can impact your physical well-being. Hate, anger and resentment can begin to manifest physically in your body. You may walk bent over, feeling the weight of your resentment on your shoulders. Bitterness or fury may well up inside of you at the mere thought of this person. Seeing this person may cause your heart to race. Your body begins living in a constant state of heightened awareness and is always on edge.

Some people will choose to bury their emotions with increased drinking or fall into a pattern of substance abuse. Our society encourages us to mask our emotions with prescription drugs. There are absolutely times when it is necessary to take prescription drugs to break a cycle of depression or to ease anxiety. Many people require daily doses of prescription medications for health reasons. I am not advocating for people who need prescription drugs to stop taking them. I am simply concerned about the prevalence of physicians prescribing pills as a quick fix for our emotions without addressing the underlying problems.

In my book, *Walking Toward the Light,* there is a scene in which I experience PVCs (premature ventricular contractions), also known as heart palpitations. I used to feel my heart flutter, and then I would sense a cramp in my heart followed by tightness in my chest. This went on for weeks before I finally went to my doctor. After some preliminary testing that showed my heart was in good shape, my physician informed me that my condition was most likely stress-induced. He immediately prescribed anti-anxiety medication for daytime and a sleeping pill for nighttime. I was under such duress at that point that I was willing to give the pills a try. Unfortunately, the anti-anxiety medication made me feel like I was walking through a fog. I could barely function. I decided it was not a good solution for me. I needed to address the reason for my stress, versus camouflaging my emotions. My resentment for my ex-husband was so deep-seated that it had begun to take its toll on me physically. This was my body's way of screaming at me to confront my feelings.

Living in a constant state of anger or resentment can lead to increased heart rate, elevated blood pressure, skin conditions or hives, just to name a few. This state can also compromise your immune system. Stress can cause elevated levels of cortisol, an adrenal hormone which rushes to your body's defense. It provides energy, reduces inflammation and controls how your body regulates fat deposits. Too much cortisol over an extended period of time can cause issues with your immune system. Many of these ailments, if left untreated, can develop into major health issues.

Continuing to hold onto resentment only damages you. The person who has hurt you has likely moved on with his or her life and may have no idea that you are harboring any ill feelings. Your emotions don't impact the person you have not forgiven. Your emotions are only impacting you and your health.

You are the only one living in a constant state of bitterness. When you look at your life through glasses tarnished with animosity or fear, your resentment can carry through to other aspects of your life. You may find it difficult to maintain and develop healthy emotional relationships with others. By rehashing past memories, you are actively living in the past and not the present. It is impossible to move forward with one foot in the past. In reality, you are the only one being hurt.

In my case, after seeking medical help and understanding that my emotions were manifesting as health issues, I made a choice to address my feelings and face the root cause of my stress.

CHAPTER THREE
Forgiveness begins with you

"Forgiveness is a gift you give yourself."
— Tony Robbins

One of the hardest concepts to understand or even accept regarding the process of forgiveness is the idea that it all starts with forgiving ourselves. I know this concept sounds ridiculous, but hear me out.

In some cases, people experience guilt regarding their role in the hurtful event. Sometimes we don't even know we are experiencing any guilt because it is buried so deep inside. The guilt may be as simple as feeling at fault for not being able to forgive this person who has harmed you.

In my case, I experienced guilt because I was the one who had initiated the divorce. I felt responsible for breaking our family apart, even though it was my ex's actions that had driven me to make such a decision. I also felt I had to accept responsibility for my part in the breakdown of our marriage. My role as a co-dependent in our relationship led to many unhealthy behaviors for me; however, my actions were my choice. I had chosen to stay in a co-dependent situation and I felt shame for not enlisting the help of a therapist earlier.

Many times victims in abuse cases will feel a sense of culpability. As a young girl, I was in a situation where I was taken advantage of and was left with guilt afterwards. Even though a crime had been perpetrated against me, I felt blameworthy for not seeing the signs. I felt regret that I had unknowingly put myself in a questionable situation. I was only 18 years old at the time, but I can still remember feeling as if somehow I had invited this crime. In order to heal, I needed to forgive, and the forgiveness began with forgiving myself for the mistakes I had made that put me in harm's way. I am not suggesting that victims of abuse should feel any responsibility for being abused, but the reality is that sometimes our emotions differ from our logic. Whether it is appropriate or not, guilt is sometimes part of the aftermath of an abuse or crime.

Holding a grudge, carrying hatred in our hearts or wishing ill-fated things to happen to our abuser can create feelings of guilt, as well. You may even experience guilt because you have been unable to forgive and move on.

Forgiving yourself is the first step on the path toward forgiveness, whether you need to forgive yourself for your perceived role in the damaging event or for just holding a grudge.

In order to begin the process of forgiving myself, I needed to acknowledge all the feelings around my divorce, my marriage and my ex-husband. This is my list:

> **Sadness** – I felt sad that I was not enough
> for him, that he didn't love me like I

loved him, and that my family was breaking apart.

Loss/Grief – I grieved over the loss of my hopes, dreams and goals for our future together. We would not grow old together. My dreams for our future were over.

Anger/Resentment – I was angry that he would not change his behavior in order to keep our family together. I resented him for not putting our family first.

Failure – I felt as if I wasn't a good enough wife/spouse.

Guilt – I felt horrible for filing for the divorce.

Now it is your turn. Please use the following pages to make a list of all the feelings associated with the event for which you are trying to forgive someone. Just concentrate on writing down the feelings for now (for example, anger, betrayal, sadness). We will revisit the list later to fill in why you are feeling each specific emotion. Remember to be as honest as you can. Write down only the feelings as they come into your thoughts.

It all starts with the question, *"How do I feel when I think about (insert your event)?"*

I FEEL....

I FEEL…

The next step is to go back and look at each feeling. Then ask yourself, "*Why am I feeling this emotion?*" Refer to my list if you need a starting point. Many of the emotions I was feeling at the time were not logical, but emotions are feelings, and the laws of logic often do not apply.

Consider why you are having each emotion. Go back to the page. Next to each feeling, describe why you are having this emotion. Be as descriptive as possible. You may even want to use a separate piece of paper. Acknowledging your feelings and their foundations is a very important step. Take your time with this exercise. We cannot change the things we don't acknowledge. Recognizing your feelings and understanding why you feel the way you feel will set the foundation for forgiveness.

CHAPTER FOUR
Stepping stones to forgiveness

"Forgiveness is the fragrance the violet sheds on the heel that has crushed it."
— Mark Twain

In the previous chapter, you have acknowledged your feelings and why you feel the way you do. You were able to create this list of feelings by replaying the movie reel of the event in your mind. However, it would be counterproductive to continue to replay the old movies. They conjure up all the feelings associated with the event: fear, sadness, anger, resentment, rage, hate and bitterness. Each time the movie reel plays, you are reliving the event. You feel like a victim all over again, and this leaves you feeling weak, exposed and preyed upon. For me, this was the most difficult part of my journey toward forgiveness.

Consider the following analogy. Have you ever rented a bad movie? You watch the entire movie and when it is finished you think, "Why did I bother watching this movie? It was horrible." You are annoyed that you have wasted your time watching something that was not enjoyable. You realize you will never have that time back. Would you ever consider watching the same "bad" movie again?

Memories of traumatic life events are "bad" movies. Consider just how many times a day, each week or each month, that you've replayed the short movie in your mind of the event that has occurred. The movie begins running as soon as an emotion triggers the replay. Your mind justifies your continued grip on the emotions you have about this event. It's exhausting watching the same old reel over and over again. It's a "bad" movie.

Spoiler alert: You know how the movie ends. The event or trauma has happened. It cannot be changed. It is over, yet you continue to rehash the event like it is happening in present time. This is extremely detrimental for the following reasons:

- Time spent watching this movie is taking time away from living in the current moment.
- Watching the scenes again and again brings up all the negative emotions associated with the event.
- You are the only one reliving the moments. The perpetrator has moved on. He or she is not replaying your movie.
- You are the only one feeling the hurt and pain over and over.
- Once the movie is done, you are left with feelings that tarnish whatever you do next, and this keeps you from living in the present moment.

In order to move forward, you have to watch the movie one last time. This time you will be an outsider reviewing the movie, breaking down the events to understand actions and emotions. When you can break the replay cycle, space will open up for positive thoughts.

This time, dissect the perpetrator's actions from your emotions. It is time to deconstruct it and capture the actions and emotions as if you are writing a script. I know this may sound crazy, but it worked for me. I have provided an example below of my process.

Very late one evening as I was in my room trying to sleep, I heard a loud crash. My ex-husband had broken something in the kitchen. There was lots of raging, yelling, cursing and banging around. My heart began to race, and the movie of his last rage while we were married came flooding back.

HIS ACTION(S)	MY FEELING(S)
Yelling at me	Fear – I don't like confrontation.
Verbally threatening	Scared – How will I take care of my kids?
	Abandoned – I thought he loved me?
	Angry – How could he say those things?

As you can see from above, often just one or two actions can create a variety of emotions.

Now it's your turn to replay the movie one last time. On the next page, use the format I have provided to capture the actions of the event and the associated feelings.

Steps to Forgiveness

HIS/HER ACTION(S)	YOUR FEELING(S)

Now comes the most difficult part of the exercise. The event has been deconstructed into two columns which are interconnected. You only have control over one column: your emotions.

Turn your attention once again to the action column. The events documented in this column are actions completed by another person. In most cases, these behaviors are a result of that person's own history, conditioning or a trauma he or she has experienced.

I have found that most bad decisions we make are a result of fear. Each one of us is a product of his or her experiences. This may be very difficult to do, but, for just a moment, put yourself in the shoes of the person who has hurt you. Is it possible his or her actions are a result of a trauma, hurt or other difficulties? Did his or her behavior originate out of fear? Can you see the fear in his or her actions?

Most people do not wake up in the morning planning to harm other people. Most people wake up each day wanting to be a thoughtful and caring person, but often fear shapes their choices.

To begin to release yourself from your emotions associated with a certain person's actions, you will need to stop judging that person for his or her behavior. It is not our responsibility to judge others. When you accept that no one is in a position to judge anyone else, this makes letting go of the judgments easier. I was able to stop judging by realizing that I am not perfect and that I do not want others to judge me; therefore, I should not judge others. The minute I stopped judging my ex-husband's actions, I broke the link between his actions and my emotions. When I could view his actions without judging them, I felt no emotion.

Nothing can change the past. The event has happened. It is done. You will not be able to live in the moment or live a happy and productive life if you are constantly living in the past. The actions, even if they were perpetrated against you, are the property of someone else. You are not responsible for that person's behavior, and you have absolutely no control over anyone else's actions. However, you can control your own emotions, the feelings listed in column two.

Your emotions are what cause you distress, not the actions of the individual. Understanding that concept will help you find the peace of true forgiveness. The trauma has already happened. It is in the past. By reliving the event, you put yourself back into the moment, and all the negative feelings come back to you. Remember, this is a "bad" movie, and it is no longer available for viewing.

I don't wish to minimize the depth of your emotions or the pain they cause; however, you are in control. You alone can elect to feel misery or contentment.

> *"When you hold resentment toward another, you are bound to that person or condition by an emotional link that is stronger than steel. Forgiveness is the only way to dissolve that link and get free."* — Katherine Ponder

Once you stop viewing the movie, the negative emotions will not be accessible because there is no image to trigger these feelings. I challenge you to never again watch the horrible scenes of this event. Now it is time to make a conscious decision to choose happiness. To embrace contentment, you need to end the pain and eliminate the adverse reactions. Once the negative feelings are gone, there will be space for positive thoughts. You can replace any negative feelings with happy ones. I recommend thinking about something that brings a smile to your face, a funny story or moment, something that elicits happiness. Eventually, you may even be able to replace negative thoughts and emotions with compassion and empathy for the person who wronged you.

Steps to stop the "bad" movies:

- Hit the STOP button.
- Choose to be happy.
- Create desire deep in your heart to attract happiness.
- Remember, you can't change the past. The individual's actions were born out of fear and his or her own past traumas.
- Release yourself from any negative emotions.
- Think about something that evokes happiness and peace.

CHAPTER FIVE
It's in your actions

"I wondered if that was how forgiveness budded; not with the fanfare of epiphany, but with pain gathering its things, packing up, and slipping away unannounced in the middle of the night."
— Khaled Hosseini, *The Kite Runner*

I never really experienced an "aha" moment in which I knew I had forgiven my ex-husband. I just noticed one day that I was calmer, happier and at peace. Sometimes I felt as though my energy was reverberating at a higher, peaceful level. It was, and still is, a daily practice and struggle to live in a state of forgiveness. It is easy to say the words, "I forgive," but they have no impact if your actions are not in line. If you have read, *Walking Toward the Light*, you know that my daily mantra of chanting "I forgive" did not work. Out of desperation, I created a framework for forgiveness that used actions as the final step on my path.

In previous chapters, you have broken down the event and made the brave decision to stop replaying the movie. You have separated "another's actions" from "your emotions." Now the challenge is to begin weaving forgiveness into everyday life and to embrace positive feelings.

The purpose of this chapter is to help you create new and positive emotions tied to physical tasks that allow you to refocus your feelings and energy whenever you begin to cue up that "bad" movie. As you incorporate happy thoughts into your daily routine, there will be no space for negative emotions. They will be pushed out by all the positive feelings you are having.

Many of us have read about the "law of attraction," the idea that what you think about manifests in your life. While I do agree with this premise, we do have a responsibility to actually *live* what we think about in order to create change. We can speak about what we want all day. The challenge is to act accordingly on a daily basis. You have to embrace your new positive feelings in your heart and pour those feelings into your routine.

Start by choosing an activity that gives you pleasure (cooking, gardening, woodworking, working out, etc.). For example, I love to cook. I enjoy cooking because it fills me with pleasure to know I am feeding my family or friends. During the last three months of caring for my ex-husband while he battled cancer, I cooked dinner every evening. I would think about how much I enjoy cooking and how much I love my family, who would eat the meal later that night. I poured love into every movement, every dice, chop and stir. I focused on performing each task with love and gratitude. These affirmations and feelings of love became embedded in the energy of the tasks I was completing.

I used this same technique as I folded laundry. With each fold of a piece of clothing I would think about how much I love my family. For example, as I folded the arm of a shirt over, I would think how fortunate I was to be able to fold clothes for them; I had my health. I focused all my thoughts on positive things: the sunny day, a funny moment, a beautiful memory or kind thought. I dislike folding laundry immensely, but I was still able to create positive thoughts and embed them into my actions. It's all about shifting your attitude.

I felt such a sense of accomplishment and fulfillment once I was done. A true shift in my emotions began each time I did anything, from cooking to laundry to taking care of my ex-husband.

It is not the work, but instead its purpose, that makes it special. As you create positive feelings surrounding your daily tasks, you'll have a new emotional well from which to draw.

Karen Todd Scarpulla

CHAPTER SIX
Feel the power

"To forgive is to set a prisoner free and discover that the prisoner was you."
— Lewis B. Smedes, *Forgive and Forget: Healing the Hurts We Don't Deserve*

Forgiveness is also about finding your personal power. In the beginning of this journey I explained that when you feel victimized, you lose your sense of power and the ability to make decisions. Only you can find your personal power. The key is to stop giving your power to someone who doesn't even realize he or she has it.

Once you take control of your emotions and begin replacing the negative movies with positive thoughts and feelings, you will begin to feel a shift in emotions. You will begin to choose positive emotions over negative ones.

Create a new movie, one where you are the hero or heroine. You have made the bravest choice possible when you choose to forgive. This movie has a happy ending with you walking with a spring in your step and with absolute grace.

We are all important beings in the universe, and that makes every action we perform important. Imagine the impact we have when we forgive. There is a shift in your own energy, which ultimately impacts the energy of the universe. Join me in living a life of grace, gratitude and forgiveness. The power is within you.

CHAPTER SEVEN
Forgiveness affirmations

I release the past. I choose to live in the present.

The past no longer affects my future.

I forgive myself for my past mistakes and release myself from any guilt.

I no longer stand in a place of judgment. I project compassion and empathy for those who have hurt me.

Today I put love into everything I do.

I choose to live in happiness, living consciously in the present moment.

I forgive those whose actions have hurt me, and I release myself from the role of victim.

I have the power to choose my own emotions.

No one has the power to make me unhappy.

Karen Todd Scarpulla

RESOURCES

Katie, Byron. *Loving What Is: Four Questions That Can Change Your Life.* New York, NY: Three Rivers, 2003. Print.

Lerner, Harriet Goldhor. *The Dance of Fear: Rising above Anxiety, Fear, and Shame to Be Your Best and Bravest Self.* New York: Perennial Currents, 2005. Print.

Young, William P., Wayne Jacobsen, and Brad Cummings. *The Shack: A Novel.* Newbury Park, CA: Windblown Media, 2007. Print.

Karen Todd Scarpulla

ABOUT THE AUTHOR

Karen lives in Chicago, Illinois, with her children. She continues to share her journey of forgiveness with audiences around the country. She is currently writing a sequel to *Walking Toward the Light* titled *Walking through the Shadows*, which follows the family's journey through the next year and the aftermath of her ex-husband's death. Order your copy of *Walking Toward the Light* on amazon. To find out about speaking engagements, visit www.walkingbeyond.com.

Karen Todd Scarpulla

LINKS

Follow Karen on social media:

Twitter: @k_scarpulla

www.facebook.com/karentoddscarpulla

Watch/Listen:

http://www.youtube.com/channel/UCCly-1RPd8xU01rY-eC4ITQ

Download the Meditation App: *Yes You Can Forgive*

iPhone: https://itunes.apple.com/us/app/yes-you-can-forgive/id763798376?ls=1&mt=8

Android: https://play.google.com/store/apps/details?id=com.clearmindsounds.android.yesyoucanforgive

www.ingramcontent.com/pod-product-compliance
Lightning Source LLC
Chambersburg PA
CBHW061311040426
42444CB00010B/2600